SPEAK

by
Laurie Halse Anderson

Teacher Guide

Written by
Pat Watson

Note

The hardcover edition, published by Farrar Straus Giroux, New York ©1999 was used to prepare this guide. Page references may differ in other editions.

Please note: Parts of this novel deal with sensitive, mature issues. Please assess the appropriateness of this book for the age level and maturity of your students prior to reading and discussing it with your class.

ISBN 1-58130-698-9

To order, contact your local school supply store, or—

Novel Units, Inc.
P.O. Box 433
Bulverde, TX 78163-0433

Web site: www.educyberstor.com

Table of Contents

Summary 3

Characters 3

Background Information 4

About the Author 5

Initiating Activities 5

Eight Sections 7
Each section contains: Summary, Vocabulary,
Discussion Questions, and Supplementary Activities

Post-reading Discussion Questions 19

Post-reading Extension Activities 23

Assessment 24

Glossary 25

Skills and Strategies

Writing
Compare/contrast, poetry, letter, sequel, TV script, dialogue, reflection

Comprehension
Cause/effect, predicting

Listening/Speaking
Discussion, dramatizing, music

Vocabulary
Target words, definitions, application

Literary Elements
Characterization, simile, analogy, metaphor, allusion, theme, alliteration, figurative language, symbolism, plot development

Thinking
Research, analysis, critical thinking

Across the Curriculum
Art—caricatures, drawing, collage

Genre: fiction

Point of View: first person

Themes: ostracism, withdrawal, isolation, aftermath of rape

Setting: Merryweather High School

Style: narrative

Summary

The protagonist of the story, Melinda Sordino, enters her freshman year at Merryweather High School as an outcast because she called the cops when she had some trouble at an end-of-summer party. Several of her friends were arrested and all became angry and turned against her. She becomes increasingly alienated and silent as the school year progresses. Her parents, who live separate lives in their own worlds, offer little help. Melinda finds solace in her art class, and an art project eventually helps her face the truth about the party. High school senior Andy Evans, whom she refers to as "IT," raped her at the party and continues to hover in the background of her life. When her tormenter again accosts her, Melinda at last finds her "voice" and her ability to defend herself. Her vindication paves the way for her recovery.

Honors: 1999 National Book Award Finalist for Young People's Literature; Parents' Guide to Children's Media Award for Outstanding Achievement; New England Children's Booksellers Association Fall Pick, Junior Library Guild Selection; Bookreporter.com Top 10 Teen Books of 1999; Booklist—Top 10 First Novels of 1999; amazon.com—Top 10 Teen Books of the Month; Fanfare—*The Horn Book's* Honor List; *School Library Journal*—Best Book of the Year.

Characters

Melinda Sordino: protagonist; freshman at Merryweather High School; ostracized by her former friends; suffers aftermath of rape

Melinda's parents: preoccupied with jobs, they both often communicate with Melinda through notes left on the kitchen counter; reflect their strained relationship and insensitivity to Melinda's needs

Students at Merryweather High

Heather: newcomer to Merryweather High; becomes Melinda's pseudo-friend who uses her when she needs her, then drops her in favor of more prestigious friends

David Petrakis: Melinda's highly intelligent biology lab partner; friendly toward her; becomes Melinda's "hero"

Rachel: Melinda's former best friend; seeks friendship with foreign-exchange students; begins to date the boy who raped Melinda

Nicole: athletic; although not formerly a close friend, she does not treat Melinda as a pariah

Ivy: friend from junior high; fellow art student who treats Melinda kindly

Andy Evans: the boy who raped Melinda, a.k.a. "IT" and "Andy Beast"; senior at Merryweather High; handsome "ladies' man"

Melinda's Teachers

Mr. Freeman: art; compassionate and helpful; reaches out and offers encouragement to Melinda

Hairwoman: English; so-named because of uncombed stringy hair drooping on her shoulders

Mr. Neck: social studies; speaks out against "reverse discrimination"

Spanish: unnamed; teaching style includes charades

Ms. Keen: biology; large; dresses in garish clothing

Mr. Stetman: algebra

Background Information

Because the protagonist experiences many of the common reactions and symptoms of post-traumatic stress disorder (PTSD) as the aftermath of rape, the following information will be beneficial as the teacher guides students in the study of this novel. Information is taken from *The Women's Complete Healthbook,* edited by Roselyn Payne Epps and Susan Cobb Stewart, ©1995 by The Philip Lief Group, Inc. and the American Medical Women's Association, and can be found at http://www.amwadoc.org/publications/WCHealthbook/violenceamwa-ch10.html.

The word "rape," from the Latin *rapere,* means "to take by force." Rape is an act of aggression in which the rapist demonstrates a need to humiliate and overpower the victim. About 80% of rapes are committed by someone the victim knows.

Reactions to the trauma of rape can include one or more of the following: repeated mental flashbacks, hypersensitivity to surroundings, strong reactions to an event or location that reminds the victim of the violence, denial that the incident happened, or repression of memories. After effects also include experiencing anger, grief, depression, anxiety, self-doubt, loss of self-esteem, lack of self-confidence, and/or loss of a sense of safety. Rape victims often blame themselves instead of the perpetrator. The stages of emotional reactions are similar to those a grief-stricken person experiences and may occur and reoccur in any sequence. These include pain, nausea, insomnia, changes in sleeping and eating patterns, and hot and cold flashes. The rape victim needs safety, comfort, and crisis counseling but often feels too afraid, ashamed, disoriented, or defiled to report the rape to anyone.

Rape statistics: about 683,000 United States women were raped in 1990; more than 12 million women have been raped at some time in their lives; every 6 minutes, a woman is raped; every 15 seconds, a woman is slapped, kicked, or otherwise abused by a man she knows; every day, approximately 4 women are murdered by a husband or boyfriend.

According to the AMWA, teenage girls are particularly vulnerable and need to understand that there is safety in numbers, to be aware of the dangers of date rape, and to recognize the necessity of establishing boundaries if a date begins to pressure them to have sex. Alcohol and drugs are often causative factors.

About the Author

Laurie Halse Anderson was born on October 23, 1961, in Potsdam, New York and grew up in Syracuse. She and her husband and two teenage daughters now live in Pennsylvania. *Speak* is her first novel; however, she previously authored three picture books: *No Time for Mother's Day, Turkey Pox,* and *Ndito Runs.* Other books by Anderson include *Fever 1793* (Fall 2000) and the Wild at Heart series (Spring & Fall 2000).

Initiating Activities

Use one or more of the following activities to introduce the novel.

1. Place the word "Isolation" on the overhead transparency. Cluster ideas around the central word: synonyms, antonyms, causes, remedies.

2. Read "Alone" or "Nothing Much" by Maya Angelou. Reference: *The Complete Collected Poems of Maya Angelou,* Random House: New York, 1994.

3. Have students write definitions for metaphor, simile, allusion, personification, and alliteration. Have them keep a record of these literary devices as they find them in the novel. The devices are listed in the supplementary activities at the end of each section of discussion questions in this guide.

Additional Information

Students are asked to write several poems during the study of the novel. Give them the following patterns:

Cinquain
Line 1: one word (noun) to give the title
Line 2: two words to describe the title
Line 3: three words to express action concerning the title
Line 4: four words to express feeling about the title
Line 5: one word that is a synonym for the title

Diamente
Line 1: one word (a noun, the subject)
Line 2: two words (adjectives describing line 1)
Line 3: three words ("-ing" or "-ed" words that relate to line 1)
Line 4: four words (first two nouns relate to line 1; second two nouns to line 7)
Line 5: three words ("-ing" or "-ed" words that relate to line 7)
Line 6: two words (adjectives describing line 7)
Line 7: one word (noun that is opposite of line 1)

Name Poem

Place the name vertically on the paper. Write adjectives or descriptive phrases about the person, using the letters to begin the first word of each line.

Five-senses
Line 1: color of the emotion
Line 2: sound of the emotion
Line 3: taste of the emotion
Line 4: smell of the emotion
Line 5: sight (what the emotion looks like)
Line 6: feeling evoked by the emotion

Pages 3-24 "Welcome to Merryweather High" through "Heathering"

The narrator, Melinda Sordino, reveals the trauma of her first two weeks as a freshman at Merryweather High School. Her friends have all turned against her, and she alludes to something that happened during the summer.

Vocabulary

obscene (3)	abstinence (4)	idiot savants (4)	fascists (4)
thespians (4)	predator (5)	indoctrination (5)	morphing (6)

Discussion Questions

1. Analyze Melinda's reaction to the first day of high school and why her fears seem more intense than that of others. Analyze why she says, "I am Outcast." *(She feels sick. No one will sit with her on the bus, and she feels she has the wrong hair, the wrong clothes, and the wrong attitude. Her ex-friends ignore her, and her former best friend mouths the words "I hate you." Something has obviously happened that has turned everyone against her. pp. 3-5)*

2. Examine the meanings of the "clans" and the prevalence of high school cliques. *(Responses will vary. Jocks: athletes; Country Clubbers: social climbers; Idiot Savants: intelligent but no common sense; Cheerleaders: popularity based on position of cheerleader; Human Waste: those who do nothing with their lives; Eurotrash: foreign exchange students; Future Fascists of America: want to overthrow the school administration; Big Hair Chix: bouffant hair styles; the Marthas: do-gooders; Suffering Artists: primarily interested in art; Thespians: members of drama club; Goths: members of a subculture favoring black clothing and dark music; Shredders: careless, destructive. p. 4)*

3. Discuss the "first ten lies they tell you in high school." Compare with first-day orientation in your school. Discuss whether or not students think Melinda's assumption that they are "lies" is valid. *(Read list aloud. Elicit student response. pp. 5-6)*

4. Examine Melinda's characterization of the teachers and what this reflects. *(She characterizes some of them by distinguishing features: English—Hairwoman; Social Studies—Mr. Neck. Spanish teacher is unnamed, indicating Melinda's lack of understanding of Spanish. She calls the art teacher, Mr. Freeman, by name because she feels more comfortable in this class. Principal Principal refers to his authority. pp. 6-7, 10, 13, 17)*

5. Discuss Mr. Freeman's approach to teaching art. Ask students to relate similar experiences in classes with this type of teaching style. *(His classroom is student-oriented, reflecting the artistic endeavors of his students and the opportunity for self-expression. He does not give rules and expectations but guides students in self-discovery and creativity. Each student will spend the school year learning how to turn one object into a piece of art. He compares their adventure in art to a journey. pp. 9-12)*

6. Discuss Melinda's home life. *(Her mother works long hours, her father is preoccupied with his own life, and the family has very little interaction. They communicate by leaving notes on the kitchen counter. Melinda's room reflects her interests as a fifth grader, but she feels that a request for change would result in an argument between her parents. pp. 14-17)*

7. Discuss the interaction between Melinda and Heather. *(She and Heather, a new student, begin a friendship by sitting together at orientation and lunch; Heather wants Melinda to join a club with her.)*

Supplementary Activities

1. Have students draw a caricature of one of the teachers based on Melinda's description.

2. Analyze the analogy on p. 9, "Art follows lunch, like dream follows nightmare." Have students write an analogy from their own experiences.

3. Note the literary devices: **Metaphors**—I (Melinda): a wounded zebra (p. 5); Vietnam or Iraq: TV wars (p. 7); flow of students: stream (p. 7); Melinda: a fish (p. 7); eyebrow maneuver: telegraph (p. 11); Melinda's room: postcard of who she was in fifth grade (p. 15); Nicole: Warrior Princess (p. 19) **Similes**—Mr. Freeman's big old grasshopper body like a stilt-walking circus guy, nose like a credit card sunk between his eyes (p. 10); clay streaks the word like dried blood (p. 10); look on his face like Daffy Duck's when Bugs is pulling a fast one (p. 17); Heather geeking around me like a moth (p. 19); black mess looks like goose poop (p. 21); dropped like a hot Pop Tart on a cold kitchen floor (p. 21)

Pages 24-46 "Burrow" through "Nightmare"

Melinda attends a pep rally where she is taunted and harassed by other students because she called the cops to an end-of-the-summer party. Tensions mount between Heather and Melinda.

Vocabulary

potpourri (26)	paparazzi (28)	synchronized (29)	inspiration (30)
expiration (30)	floundering (31)	blathers (33)	interim (35)
drones (39)	ecology (41)	steroid (41)	irony (43)

Discussion Questions

1. Discuss Melinda's "place of refuge" and how she describes it. *(While trying to avoid her social studies teacher, Melinda steps into an old janitor's closet. With its old furnishings and isolation, it is the perfect retreat for Melinda because it is abandoned, has no purpose, and no name. This is exactly the way Melinda feels. pp. 25-26)*

2. Examine what happens to Melinda during the first pep rally and what the events reveal. Ask students why they think Melinda called the cops at the party. *(She goes only because Heather insists. A girl calls her by name and announces that she is the one who called the cops at the party. Others speak up of arrests and embarrassment because of Melinda, but she is unable to tell them what really happened. She is harassed by girls jamming their knees into her back and yanking her hair and is knocked down three rows of bleachers as the pep rally ends. pp. 26-30)*

3. Discuss the significance of Melinda's painting for a week after the pep rally. *(Melinda paints watercolors of trees that have been hit by lightning. The trees are nearly, but not totally, dead. One picture is so dark the tree is barely visible. These trees symbolize Melinda: she feels she has been struck by something as terrible as lightning and that it has left her barely alive. Some days are worse than others. pp. 30-31)*

4. Contrast the homes and families of Heather and Melinda. *(Heather: mother there, makes hot chocolate for the girls, wants Heather to invite friends, room is beautifully decorated and organized, has her own TV and phone, reflects her personality. Melinda: mother rarely there, room disorganized and outdated, has no personality. pp. 32-33)*

5. Analyze Melinda's confrontation with her parents over her grades. Ask students how their parents would react. *(All "role-play": father stern and demanding; mother vacillates between sympathetic and severe; Melinda, the Victim. Melinda's parents have received interim reports revealing Melinda's low grades. Her parents are angry and demand that she get her grades up. Melinda retreats, leaving her parents arguing. pp. 35-36)*

6. Trace significant events in Melinda's life following the confrontation with her parents. *(Rachel humiliates her in algebra class; she is alone on Halloween night, troubled by memories of the previous Halloween with her friends; she is embarrassed in Spanish class; Heather joins the Martha clan and enlists Melinda's help; she overhears other "Marthas" talking about her and cries. pp. 37-45)*

7. Analyze the significance of Melinda's nightmare about IT. Ask students what they think IT symbolizes. *(IT is obviously a person who symbolizes the trauma Melinda has experienced. She encounters IT at school, but she feels she must never tell anyone what happened. pp. 45-46)*

8. **Prediction:** Will Melinda continue to remain silent about what happened at the party?

Supplementary Activities

1. Have students write a poem or a paragraph that explains what they think "IT" represents.

2. Literary devices: **Metaphors**—pad of late passes: get-out-of-jail free cards (p. 26); silence at pep rally: block of ice (p. 28); promiscuous cheerleaders on Saturday night: virginal goddesses on Monday (p. 29); Trinity (God the Father, Son, and Holy Spirit): Visa, MasterCard, American Express (p. 29); Melinda: the Victim (p. 35); parents: tall ghosts in khakis (p. 40) **Similes**— throat squeezes shut as if two hands of black fingernails are clamped on windpipe (p. 28); stain on carpet looks like algae (p. 34); Dad snorts like a bull (p. 36); Ms. Keen would look like a tiny grandmother doll; she must look like a basketball (p. 37). **Allusion**—Martha, noted for good deeds (p. 43): Bible, Luke 10:38-41; also Martha Stewart, craft guru, "the lady who writes books about cheery decorations."

Pages 49-68 "Go _________ (Fill in the Blank)!" through "First Amendment, Second Verse"

Melinda continues to take refuge in her "closet." Her physical problems increase. Tensions between her parents continue. Mr. Freeman, the art teacher, encourages her.

Vocabulary

Eurocentric (49)	patriarchs (49)	warp (51)	mortuary (52)
immigration (53)	xenophobic (56)	subjectivity (61)	anthropologist (62)
stamens (65)	pistils (65)	hypothalamus (65)	

Discussion Questions

1. Discuss Melinda's decline, including physical symptoms. *(When her parents require her to stay after school for extra help from teachers, Melinda retreats to her closet. This becomes like a fort to her, offering protection. It is becoming more difficult for her to talk; her throat is always sore and her lips are raw from biting them. Clenched jaws lead to a daily headache. She occasionally talks to Heather, but freezes up when trying to talk to her parents or teachers. She longs to confess everything but is unable to do so and knows the memory will remain forever. pp. 50-51)*

2. Note reference to Maya Angelou on p. 50 and refer back to poems "Alone" and "Nothing Much" mentioned in Initiating Activities section (page 5 of this guide).

3. Analyze the social studies class "debate" and its aftermath. Note who challenges the teacher and the position each person takes. Ask the students how they feel about this type of debate, if the teacher is right or wrong, and if a student has the right to challenge a teacher. *(The teacher is angry because he believes immigration and "reverse discrimination" have kept his son from getting a job as firefighter. He asks the students to debate whether or not America should have closed her borders in 1900. Several students realize this would have kept their grandparents or parents from entering the United States, and the ensuing arguments are heated. David Petrakis, an excellent student who is never in trouble, challenges the teacher's right to limit the debate to those who agree with his viewpoint. David walks out of the room and later begins to record the class sessions after his parents threaten a lawsuit. He becomes Melinda's "hero" for standing up for what is right. pp. 53-57, 66-68)*

4. Discuss the Thanksgiving dinner for Melinda's family and why this is significant. *(Her mother is consumed with business problems but attempts to cook a turkey. Her parents argue over the turkey, her mother leaves to go to her business, and her father's attempts at preparing a meal end in disaster. They order in pizza. The events symbolize further deterioration of the family relationships and the parents' misplaced priorities. pp. 57-61)*

Supplementary Activities

1. In small groups, have students find information about and discuss their school mascot. Group 1: Name the mascot and tell why this is appropriate for the school. Group 2: Research when the name was chosen and whether or not it has always been the same. If it has changed, why? Group 3: Draw different logos that represent the mascot. Group 4: Write a rhyme about the mascot.

2. Melinda retreats from her problems, yet admires David for standing up to Mr. Neck. Have students record Melinda's coping strategies using examples from the novel and create lists of possible alternative strategies. Stress the importance of recognizing and evaluating options.

3. Literary devices: **Metaphors**—Melinda's trauma at the party: beast in her gut (p. 51); Mr. Neck: a bull (p. 53); the turkey: iceberg (p. 58); argument: few bubbles splashing on the stove (p. 59); Melinda: bird (62); turkey skeleton: hideous sacrifice (p. 62); Ninth grade: zit-cream commercial (p. 66); seed: white hand (p. 67) **Similes**—Melinda's preparations in her closet like building a fort (p. 50); Melinda's mother setting unrealistic goals for her store: like watching someone caught in an electric fence (p. 57); Thanksgiving dinner is like a holy obligation (p. 58); long curly cord snakes around like a rope tying her to the stake (p. 59); Mr. Neck's voice as smooth as a new-poured road (p. 67)

Pages 69-92 "Wombats Rule!" through "Dark Art"

Christmas vacation brings Melinda little relief from her tormenting thoughts. Art class continues to be a bright spot in her school day. The relationship between Heather and Melinda deteriorates. IT, now named as Andy Evans, continues to haunt Melinda.

Vocabulary

wombat (69)	imperial (69)	demure (75)	vermilion (78)
capitalists (84)	dormant (87)	abysmal (89)	fluorescent (90)
fungal (92)			

Discussion Questions

1. Analyze Melinda's statement about her parents, "I bet they'd be divorced by now if I hadn't been born." Ask what this reflects about her self-esteem. (*She blames herself for their unhappiness and believes that, if not for her, they would be divorced and going on with their lives. She feels she must be a disappointment to them, not pretty or athletic, just ordinary. She does not find anything positive about herself. p. 70*)

2. Examine Melinda's references to her secret and what this reveals about her relationship with her parents. Ask students what they think happened at the party. (*On Christmas Day, touched by the fact that they have noticed her drawing, she almost tells them her secret. She feels as if there is a snowball in her throat that keeps getting larger and prevents her from speaking. She knows they suspect she was at the party. She remembers that they thought she was at Rachel's for the night and when she crept home after the party, both cars were gone, her mother didn't return until 2 a.m., and her dad at sunup. She cannot find a place to start and the moment is lost; Student response concerning what happened will vary. Note a key point, "I showered until the hot water was gone, then I crawled in bed and did not sleep." Rape victims often want to wash away the pain and degradation. p. 72*)

3. Discuss Melinda's athletic ability, her attitude toward being on the basketball team, and the comparison she makes between basketball and life. (*She demonstrates unusual ability in throwing foul shots. The coach checks Melinda's grades and mentions tutoring. Melinda has no intention of being on the basketball team, believing that both basketball and life knock you around and you don't get to pay either back. She doesn't tell the coaches she won't teach Brendan Keller how to throw fouls, but decides she just won't show up. pp. 75-77*)

4. Analyze the deterioration of the relationship between Melinda and Heather. (*Heather is consumed with becoming part of the Martha clan and has time for Melinda only when she needs her. Melinda reluctantly agrees to help Heather with Martha art projects. Heather begins to model at a department store and asks Melinda to go with her for a photography shoot. The Marthas criticize Melinda's work on the poster project, and Heather fails to speak up for her. As Heather becomes more accepted by the Martha clan, Melinda slips further from her consideration. pp. 79-85, 88-89*)

5. Examine Melinda's reference to IT. *(Melinda is hanging the posters for Heather when IT creeps up behind her and whispers "Freshmeat." She is terrified because IT has found her again and she can no longer ignore him. She runs away, realizing he remembers and knows all about her. IT is identified as Andy Evans when he enters the lunchroom. pp. 85-86, 89-90)*

6. Discuss the school conference with Melinda's parents and the aftermath. Elicit student reaction to Melinda's suicide attempt, what it indicates, and what they think about her mother's reaction. *(Her parents are furious over her declining grades, and they keep questioning what is wrong with her. Melinda says nothing, believing they don't want to hear anything she has to say. She is grounded indefinitely. After showing them her completed homework, she makes a half-hearted attempt at suicide by scratching her wrists. When her mother sees the wrist, she says she doesn't have time for this and that suicide is for cowards. Students should note Melinda's cry for help and her mother's cold reaction. pp. 86-88)*

Supplementary Activities

1. Note the use of the word "drone" on p. 70 and compare with "drones" on p. 39. *(p. 70: lazy idler; p. 39: talk in a monotonous voice)*

2. As a class, discuss the effectiveness of the author not naming Melinda's "IT" until page 69.

3. Have students write a simile or metaphor about "despair."

4. Note alliteration on p. 69 about the Wombats. Have students write an alliterative description of their school mascot.

5. Literary devices: **Metaphors**—Melinda: drone (p. 70); Melinda's emotions: snowball in her throat (p. 72); Brendan Keller's arm: skinny octopus tentacle (p. 76); Melinda: trained seal (p. 76); Melinda's parents: volcanoes (p. 87); Andy Evans: Prince of Darkness (p. 90); Mr. Freeman: a blue broken cricket husk (p. 91) **Similes**—heart clangs like a fire bell (p. 71); the other employees watch me like I'm a rat (p. 73); her skin color...like underwear washed so many times it's about to fall apart (p. 73); anger whistles out of me like I'm a popped balloon (p. 74); art room blooming like a museum (p. 77); Heather looks like our Thanksgiving turkey wearing a blue bikini (p. 83); Mr. Stetman like a grandfather who wants to fix up two young kids (p. 84); peanut butter molds to roof of mouth like retainer (p. 89) **Allusion**—Second Coming (p. 87), Biblical prophecy of return of Jesus Christ to earth at the end of the age in book of Revelation

Pages 95-116 "Death of the Wombat" through "Clash of the Titans"

Seeing Andy Evans causes Melinda to skip school. Heather dissolves her friendship with Melinda and adds insult to injury on Valentine's Day. Melinda's parents are called to school for another conference.

Vocabulary

marsupials (95)	papier-mâché (95)	brunch (96)	conundrum (98)
compromise (103)	funk (103)	imbeciles (103)	tenure (104)
vespiary (104)	conjugate (107)	dynamics (114)	

Discussion Questions

1. Discuss what precipitates Melinda's skipping school and what she does. *(After missing the bus, she has to walk to school and decides to go by the bakery for a doughnut. She sees Andy Evans and runs away when he comes toward her. She decides to skip school and spends the day at the mall. pp. 96-99)*

2. Analyze the reference to the symbols in *The Scarlet Letter* and how Melinda would adapt the letter "A." *(This gives additional clues to the trauma that Melinda experienced the night of the party. Melinda refers to the symbolism of guilt, wonders if Hester tried to say no, and believes they could get along. She would change the letter to "S" for silent, stupid, scared, silly, and shame. pp. 100-101)*

3. Discuss the dissolution of Melinda and Heather's friendship and the effect it has on Melinda. Elicit student response to the meaning of friendship. *(Heather tells Melinda that they paired up at the beginning of the year because she was new but that they are very different and were never really friends. She mentions Melinda's depression and reputation and suggests that she needs professional help. Although Melinda had not seriously thought of Heather as her one true friend, she feels desperate and rejected. Heather leaves her sitting alone and joins the Marthas. On Valentine's Day, Heather adds insult to injury when she leaves a Valentine taped to Melinda's locker. Inside the Valentine is the friendship necklace Melinda gave Heather for Christmas. pp. 104-107)*

4. Analyze the events and effects of Valentine's Day on Melinda and the aftermath. *(She thinks the Valentine taped to her locker might be from David Petrakis. Although unsure about whether or not she wants him to like her, she realizes she just wants anyone to do so. She and David interact in a friendly way. When she discovers the Valentine is from Heather, she again skips school, this time spending the day in various waiting rooms of a hospital. Her truancy leads to a conference with her parents, the principal, and the guidance counselor. The guidance counselor hints at possible family problems, and her parents react in anger and frustration and reveal the underlying tension between them. Melinda remains mute, feels she is nothing, and longs to escape. Melinda is placed in In-School Suspension. pp. 107-116)*

Supplementary Activities

1. Have students complete the phrase "Friendship is..." or write a five-senses poem about "rejection."

2. Literary devices: **Metaphors**—Melinda: BunnyRabbit (p. 97); *The Scarlet Letter:* skeleton (p. 100); dark blue color: blood of imbeciles, Confusion, Tenure, etc. (p. 104); cafeteria: giant sound stage (p. 104); Melinda: small ant (p. 104); Melinda's hurt: knife (p. 111)
   Similes—snow...settles on the rooftops like powdered sugar on a gingerbread town (p. 96); it's (skipping school) like living in an MTV video (p. 98); it's (mall) supposed to be there like milk in the refrigerator or God (p. 98); notes of love and betrayal passed as if lab tables were lanes on Cupid's Highway (p. 109); smiles and blushes like tiny sparrows (p. 109)
   Allusion—wolfsmiles, showing oh granny what big teeth you have (p. 97), "Little Red Riding Hood"

Pages 116-137 "MISS" through "A Night to Remember"

When Melinda is placed in In-School Suspension, Andy Evans is there, also. Mr. Freeman "opens the door" for Melinda to talk to him. Melinda's self-image continues to decline. Her narration reveals the truth: Andy Evans raped her at the party in August.

Vocabulary

bigoted (117)	misdemeanor (117)	felony (117)	hydrochloric (117)
cubism (119)	classical (121)	germination (125)	asphyxiated (126)
wistful (129)			

Discussion Questions

1. Discuss what happens when Melinda is placed in In-School Suspension. Ask students how they would react in a similar situation. *(Andy Evans is also there, and Melinda becomes petrified. Andy blows in her ear. pp. 116-118)*

2. Analyze Mr. Freeman's effect on Melinda, inside and outside the art class. Ask students if they agree or disagree with his statement, "When people don't express themselves, they die one piece at a time." *(After telling her that her imagination is paralyzed, Mr. Freeman gives her a book featuring the work of Picasso. This opens a door of understanding for Melinda. When Melinda is walking to her mother's store in the snow, Mr. Freeman gives her a ride. They begin to talk about the emotion in art work, and he stresses that people will die if they don't express themselves. He affirms her as a "good kid" with a lot to say and offers to be there if she ever needs to talk. pp. 118-123)*

3. Examine Melinda's self-image and her survival techniques after Heather's rejection. *(As she shops, Melinda realizes she has gained weight and hates her appearance. She hates everything she tries on and realizes how pitiful she looks in the mirror. She feels totally alone and rejected by everyone except Mr. Freeman. She longs to become normal again but feels she is a loser. Survival techniques include taking her lunch so she won't have to go through the cafeteria line, trying to read while eating alone, pretending she is a scientist on the outside looking in, and imagining Heather in ten years. pp. 123-128)*

4. Examine Melinda's revelation about the night of the party and its residual effect on her. *(She was at an end-of-summer cheerleader party with beer, seniors, and music. She was entranced when Andy began to talk to and flirt with her, but his actions became sexually aggressive. He kissed her, asked her if she "wanted to," then raped her. She attempted to tell him no and that she had to leave, but he overpowered her. She saw a telephone and called 911 because she needed help, the cops came, and Melinda then walked home to an empty house. Because of her fear, she rejects David's invitation to his house for pizza after a basketball game victory. pp. 131-136)*

Supplementary Activities

1. Have students list synonyms for "fear," then write a cinquain poem about one of the words.

2. Note the figurative language, "I close the door" in Melinda's response to Mr. Freeman's offer of a listening ear (p. 123). Have students write a short poem or song lyrics beginning with this phrase, or create a drawing or painting based on this statement.

3. Literary devices: **Metaphors**—Mr. Neck: guard dog (p. 117); students in suspension: convicts (p. 117); Melinda's mother: a rock (p. 120); Melinda: the ocean (p. 120); Effert's store: fashion graveyard (p. 124); Melinda's mother and father, Rachel, the school, Heather: thornbushes (p. 125); losers: prunes in the oatmeal of school (p. 128); David: a loose ball racing downhill (p. 131); Andy Evans: a boulder (p. 135) **Similes**—a lamp that buzzes like an angry hive (p. 117); sits like a graniteboy waiting for a chisel (p. 117); I sit like I have an egg in my mouth (p. 117); get in, buy, get out, like ripping off a Band-Aid (p. 120); carcasses rot until skin hangs like ribbons over their bones (p. 121); art without emotion is like chocolate cake without sugar (p. 122); they are chewing me alive like an infestation of thoughts, shame, mistakes (p. 125); the lights like stars strung in the pines (p. 134); shadows looked like photo negatives (p. 135); sitting on porch roof like a frozen gargoyle (p. 136) **Personification**—fat white seed (cloud) sleeps in the sky (p. 133); the moon is asleep (p. 136)

Pages 141-168 "Exterminators" through "Real Spring"

Melinda's inner turmoil increases when she discovers that Rachel is dating Andy Evans. School conflicts continue. A chance encounter with Andy causes Melinda to mentally relive the rape.

Vocabulary

tenacious (142)	database (142)	profoundly (143)	genetics (146)
dominant (148)	recessive (148)	bichon frise (149)	muse (152)
suffragettes (154)	incriminate (157)	quantum physics (158)	ciao (162)
delinquency (163)			

Discussion Questions

1. Discuss the evolvement of the name of the Merryweather High School's mascot and the debate over each name. *(Trojans [p. 40]: discarded because of concern over abstinence message; Blue Devils [41]: discarded post-Halloween because of school board concern about devils; Tigers [49]: discarded due to Ecology Club protests; Wombats [69]: discarded because the wombat is a foreign animal and new uniforms would be too expensive; Hornets [95, 141]: protest against because of play on words "Horny Hornets," but no definite action taken.)*

2. Discuss the interaction between Melinda and Ivy. *(A mutual interest in art draws Melinda and Ivy together. Ivy encourages Melinda and reaches out in friendship. pp. 145-146)*

3. Have a student read aloud "Ten More Lies..." on p. 148. Ask students if they agree or disagree. *(Responses will vary.)*

4. Analyze Melinda's inner turmoil when she learns that Rachel is dating Andy. Discuss Melinda's final decision and ask students what they would do in a similar situation. *(Melinda can't escape the arguments in her mind. Thoughts of the current year mingle with past years, but she is genuinely concerned about Rachel and remembers the friendship they have shared since childhood. She debates whether or not to tell Rachel or one of her friends and decides to write Rachel an anonymous note warning her to be careful because Andy is not what he pretends to be. pp. 149-152)*

5. Examine Melinda's attempt to raise her social studies grade, the result, and whether or not the students think the teacher acts fairly. *(As an extra-credit project, she writes a report about suffragettes, spending time and effort to write the best report she's ever done. She hands it in on time, but the teacher tells her she must deliver it orally. Because Melinda has not yet "found her voice," she mimeographs copies and distributes them to the other students. She attempts to make a statement about choosing not to speak. The teacher refuses to accept this, gives her a "D" on her report, and Melinda winds up back in In-School Suspension. David Petrakis consoles her but tells her she must learn to speak up for herself. pp. 149-159)*

6. Discuss Melinda's encounter with Andy in the art room and her ensuing daydream about encounters with talk show hosts. *(She feels safe in the art room, but Andy enters, turns off the lights, and asks if she has seen Rachel. Andy seems menacing, and Melinda is unable to speak. Rachel arrives and interrupts the scene, but Melinda, terrified, immediately goes home. Shortly afterward, while home sick, she imagines herself on a TV talk show such as "Oprah," and replays the rape in her mind. In her daydream, each of the talk show hosts reassures her that it was rape and that Andy is to blame for the attack. pp. 160-165)*

Supplementary Activities

1. Analyze the symbolism of Mr. Freeman's statement, "...trees are flexible, so they don't snap. Scar it, give it a twisted branch—perfect trees don't exist...Be the tree" (p. 153). Have students respond in a poem or paragraph beginning with one of the lines.

2. Literary devices: **Alliteration**—horny Hornet heinies (p. 141) **Metaphors**—student body: hive (p. 142); rusty cars: winter rats (p. 142); Andy Evans: the Beast (p. 149); Melinda's closet: her throne room (p. 150); women: dolls (p. 154); Melinda's mental turmoil: avalanche (p. 157); Melinda: little rabbit (p. 160); Melinda: deer frozen in headlights (p. 161); mother's hand: island on Melinda's forehead (p. 163) **Allusions**—thumbs up or thumbs down (p. 142), historical reference to Roman gladiator fights; Alice in Wonderland (p. 144); Noah (p. 165), Biblical **Similes**—voice sounds like a cold engine that won't turn over (p. 146); she follows, panting like a bichon frise (p. 149); cold air...slipping like silver mercury down lungs (p. 151); ice-cream voice like a kindergarten teacher (p. 153); insides feel like caught in a tornado (p. 155); papers trembling as if breeze blowing through closed door (p. 156); leaves stick together like floppy pages in decomposing book (p. 166)

Pages 168-198 "Fault!" through "Final Cut"

Melinda begins to recover some of her self-esteem. When she discovers that Rachel is planning to go as Andy's date to the prom, she tells Rachel about the rape. Rachel is sympathetic but becomes angry when Melinda tells her Andy was the perpetrator. Andy corners her in her school "closet," and she finally finds her voice to scream "No," and to defend herself. Her narration ends on a note of hope for recovery.

Vocabulary

graffiti (175)	indentured servitude (177)	detonate (180)	perverts (186)
dormancy (188)	shards (195)	mural (196)	

Discussion Questions

1. Analyze how Melinda begins to assert herself and to "find her voice." *(Melinda proves efficient against Nicole, the best tennis player, and begins to feel more positive about herself. She determines to improve, a positive sign of improving self-esteem. She interacts more readily with Ivy. She writes Andy Evans' name on the bathroom wall with a warning to stay away from him. She refuses to help Heather with another Martha project. She resolves to talk to Rachel about the rape and realizes she must face some of her "demons." pp. 169-180)*

2. Examine Melinda's decision to talk to Rachel and the result. *(Realizing she must face the reality of the rape and in an attempt to warn Rachel, Melinda sits with her in the library. They begin to converse, and Melinda writes notes explaining what happened to her the night of the party. Rachel is sympathetic at first but calls Melinda a liar and accuses her of being jealous when Melinda tells her the perpetrator was Andy Evans. pp. 180-184)*

3. Discuss what the entries under Melinda's initial graffiti about Andy Evans reveal. *(Other girls have obviously had unpleasant sexual encounters with him and record their own warnings against him. Melinda feels justified and relieved that others, too, know the truth about Andy. pp. 185-186)*

4. Correlate Mr. Sordino's treatment and explanation of the diseased tree with Melinda's "survival." *(He tells Melinda that the tree is dying and must be cut back to a stump if it is to survive. Cutting off the diseased branches makes it possible for the tree to grow and be strong again. Following their conversation, Melinda returns to the farm where the rape occurred. She realizes that, although confused and damaged, she has survived. She cannot cut away the memories and fears, but discovers a "seed" of the former Melinda and decides she will care for that seed. Elated, she returns home, ready to live again. pp. 186-189)*

5. Analyze the aftermath of the prom. *(Melinda discovers that Andy got drunk, he and Rachel argued, and Rachel broke up with him. Melinda goes to her "closet" to retrieve her things, and Andy enters behind her and locks the door. He lashes out at her, tells her the incident was not a rape, and becomes physically and sexually aggressive. Melinda at first cannot speak, but finds her voice and begins to scream and defend herself. He hits her, and she breaks the mirror and grabs a shard of glass. As she holds the glass against his throat, he becomes paralyzed with fright. Nicole and others enter, and someone runs for help. pp. 190-195)*

6. Discuss the denouement. Note the symbolism of Melinda's final portrayal of her tree in art class. *(Melinda's tree takes on life, with one sick branch, roots coming out of the ground, and the crown reaching for the sun. Symbolically, the new growth is the best part, just as Melinda's new growth promises her return to health. Other students know about Andy's attack and affirm Melinda, and Rachel has called her. Melinda acknowledges to herself that Andy Evans raped her when she was drunk and too young to know what was happening but she realizes it was not her fault. Mr. Freeman again offers his listening ear, and Melinda replies, "Let me tell you about it." pp. 196-198)*

Supplementary Activities

1. As a class, write two name poems about Melinda: one that describes her before the rape, one that describes her after the rape.

2. Have students write a five-senses poem about either the loss of trust or regained trust, relating to Melinda's emotions.

3. Literary devices: **Similes**—bounce the ball up in the air like releasing a bird or apple (p. 170); I look like a dog chasing its tail (p. 173); graffiti on bathroom walls like a community chat room (p. 175); Melinda's dashed hopes like smelling perfect Christmas feast and having door slammed in face (p. 185) **Metaphors**—Melinda's question about Andy's departure for college: an arrow to Rachel's soft spot (p. 181); Rachel's coolness: cold front (p. 182); secret of rape: dirt (p. 183); tree trimmer: chain-saw murderer (p. 187); angry Marthas: swarm of bees (p. 191); Melinda's inability to speak: block of ice in her throat (p. 198)

Post-reading Discussion Questions

Responses to questions in this section will vary but should include information students have gained through previous discussion questions, their answers to student questions, and their reading of the book.

1. Place the graphic for a Story Map (page 21 of this guide) on an overhead transparency. Elicit response from students and fill in chart.

2. Place the graphic for Character Interaction (page 22 of this guide) on an overhead transparency. Discuss the interaction between Melinda/Andy Evans; Melinda/Rachel; Melinda/Heather; Melinda/David Petrakis, Melinda/Mr. Freeman; Melinda/her parents.

3. Discuss the physical and emotional symptoms of rape and post-traumatic stress disorder (see Background Information, page 4 of this guide) and correlate with symptoms Melinda experiences. Trace Melinda's physical decline. (Note pp. 16-17, 24-26, 28, 30, 35-36, 45, 63, 72, 81, 98, 114, 123, 127, 131, 157, 159, 164.)

4. Discuss the things that happen to Melinda that make her feel that she is a "slick nothing." (Note pp. 3-4, 14, 22, 26-30, 33-34, 40-41.)

5. Discuss Melinda's parents and her home life. Analyze what might have been different if her parents had been home the night of the rape, or if her parents had been available and supportive after her ordeal.

6. Discuss methods of effective, esteem-building parenting and correlate with Melinda's parents. Create a T-chart to record examples. How might an ineffective parent become effective or vice versa?

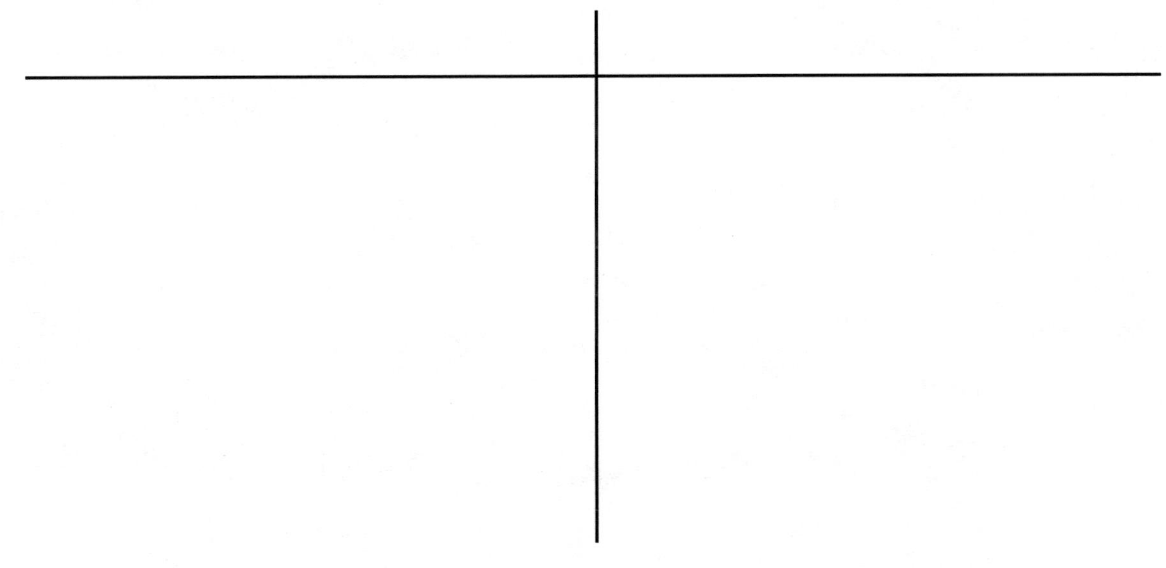

7. Discuss how Melinda's tree art project correlates with her trauma. (Note pp. 30-32, 78, 92, 119, 146-147, 151-153, 196-198.)

8. Discuss Melinda's "dialogue" with others and how often she symbolizes herself by writing "Me:" with no words. (Note pp. 9, 21, 166, 167.)

9. Discuss the portrayal of characters' "voices"; e.g. David Petrakis: silence or carefully chosen words, tape records class sessions; Mr. Freeman: the painting of school board members; Melinda: silence.

10. Discuss Melinda's hints about her real problem. (Note pp. 5, 28, 42, 45, 72, 74, 81-82, 86, 90, 97, 99, 101, 117.)

11. Discuss Melinda's relationship with David Petrakis.

12. Read Maya Angelou's poem, "Caged Bird" and correlate with Melinda's final touch to her tree art project (pp. 197-198). What do Melinda's birds symbolize?

13. Analyze the title and discuss whether or not it reflects the content of the novel.

Story Map

Directions: Use the diagram below with a partner or small group to free-associate thoughts about the novel after you have finished reading it. Jot down your thoughts in a similar format on a large piece of paper.

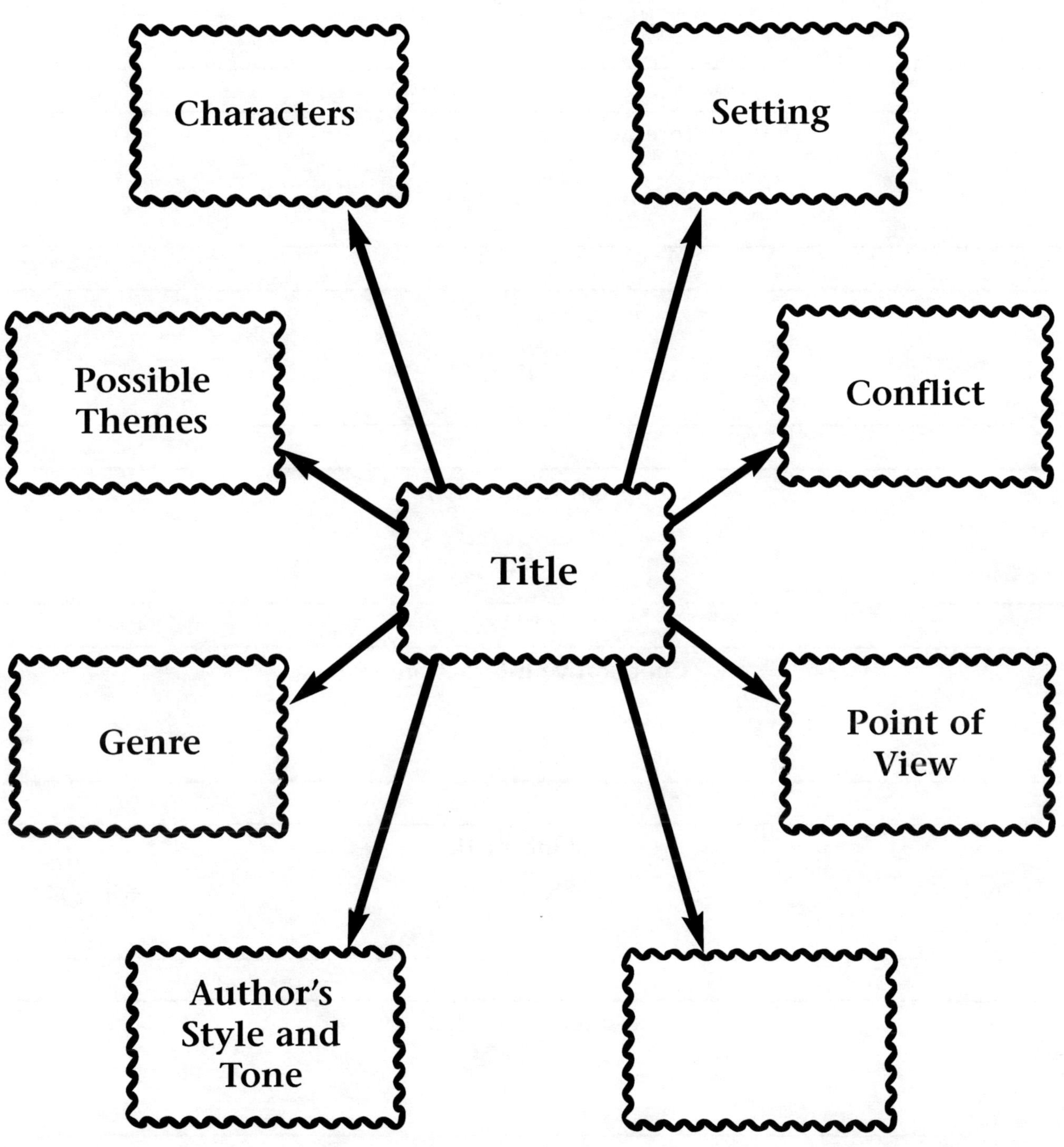

Character Interaction Chart

Conflicting Characters

Interaction of Characters

Source of Conflict

Compromise Interactions

Cooperative Interactions

Control Interactions

Results of Conflict

Post-reading Extension Activities

Note: Instructions for extensions are directed toward students. Give each student a copy and let him or her choose one or two for response.

Writing

1. Write a Public Service Announcement designed to be read on radio or television. Direct the message toward (1) parents to encourage them to reach out to and be sensitive toward their teenagers and/or to recognize signs of abuse; or (2) teenagers to tell them where to go to get help if they have been abused. The PSA should be one to one and one-half minutes long. If designed for television, suggest graphics that could be used in addition to the announcement.

2. Write a diamente poem contrasting Ostracism and Acceptance.

3. Write a sequel to the novel. Tell what happens to Andy and to Melinda.

4. Express Melinda's "nightmare" in a poem beginning with "I see a face..."

5. Write a letter from Melinda to Andy.

Drama

1. Write and stage a courtroom scene in which Andy is on trial.

2. Choose a segment from the novel and rewrite as a TV script. Perform for the class.

3. Write a monologue Melinda presents after she has found her "voice." Choose appropriate background music and read the monologue to the class.

4. Read one of Maya Angelou's poems to the class, accompanied by appropriate background music. Suggestions: "Caged Bird," "Alone," "Nothing Much."

5. Write and perform for the class a final dialogue between Melinda and Andy.

Art

1. Draw a sequence of trees representative of those Melinda draws in art class.

2. Create a collage depicting the incidents and emotions Melinda experiences.

Assessment for *Speak*

Assessment is an ongoing process. The following ten items can be completed during the novel study. Once finished, the student and teacher will check the work. Points may be added to indicate the level of understanding.

Name ____ Date ___________________

Student   **Teacher**

_______   _______   1. Correct all quizzes and tests taken over the novel.

_______   _______   2. Identify conflict (person vs. self, person vs. person, etc.) and support with passages and page numbers from the novel.

_______   _______   3. Evaluate the author's use of humor in a novel dealing with a dark subject. Write a short essay explaining why humor is or is not effective.

_______   _______   4. Share your extension project on the assigned day.

_______   _______   5. Identify literary devices as the teacher reads them aloud.

_______   _______   6. Write the correct name of a character as the teacher reads a short description aloud.

_______   _______   7. Write two review questions over the novel and participate in conducting an oral review.

_______   _______   8. Write a name poem about a character from the novel. Share your poem with the class.

_______   _______   9. Write one five-senses poem about "depression" and one about "healing."

_______   _______   10. Write a book review. Would you recommend this book? Why or why not?

Glossary

Pages 3-46

1. obscene (3): indecent, offensive

2. abstinence (4): keep or refrain from

3. idiot savants (4): mentally retarded persons who exhibit genius in a highly specialized area

4. fascists (4): persons who follow totalitarian dictatorship; reactionary persons

5. thespians (4): of or having to do with drama

6. predator (5): one who preys upon another

7. indoctrination (5): state of being taught a doctrine, belief, or principle

8. morphing (6): changing, transforming

9. potpourri (26): a fragrant mixture of dried flower petals and spices

10. paparazzi (28): freelance photographers or reporters who pursue celebrities to take candid pictures

11. synchronized (29): happening at the same time

12. inspiration (30): breathing in; creative force or influence

13. expiration (30): breathing out; dying away; coming to an end

14. floundering (31): struggling; proceeding in a bungling or hesitant manner

15. blathers (33): talks foolishness; speaks nonsense

16. interim (35): meantime; temporary; intervening

17. drones (39): talks in a monotonous tone

18. ecology (41): science devoted to the system of interrelationships between organisms and their environments

19. steroid (41): any one of a large class of structurally related compounds containing the carbon ring of the sterols; includes various hormones and acids

20. irony (43): words used with an inner meaning; speech in which meaning is opposite of that actually expressed

Pages 49-92

1. Eurocentric (49): centered around pride in European background or heritage

2. patriarchs (49): rulers of a family; venerable old men

3. warp (51): to move; to leave one's proper route

4. mortuary (52): of, or for, burial

5. immigration (53): coming into a country as a settler

6. xenophobic (56): morbidly fearful of strangers or foreign peoples

7. subjectivity (61): absorption in one's own mental state or process; tendency to view things through one's own individuality

8. anthropologist (62): one who makes a scientific study of the human race

9. stamens (65): male organs of flowering plants

10. pistils (65): female organs of a flowering plant, consisting of ovary, style, stigma

11. hypothalamus (65): part of the brain controlling temperature, hunger, thirst, and the pituitary gland

12. wombat (69): Australian marsupial resembling the opossum

13. imperial (69): of an empire; majestic

14. demure (75): reserved, quiet, staid; affecting to be grave or decorous

15. vermilion (78): bright red color or pigment

16. capitalists (84): advocates of capitalism, a system dependent on privately-owned property and profit

17. dormant (87): not acting; in a state of suspension

18. abysmal (89): miserable; too deep or great to be measured; extremely bad

19. fluorescent (90): glowing in the dark; giving off light by a substance exposed to x-ray, ultraviolet rays, or certain other rays

20. fungal (92): relating to something that grows or springs up rapidly; diseased, spongy growth

Pages 95-137

1. marsupials (95): animals that carry their young in a pouch

2. papier-mâché (95): paper pulp shaped by molding, then dried hard

3. brunch (96): combination of breakfast and lunch

4. conundrum (98): riddle, especially one with a double meaning

5. compromise (103): meeting halfway; coming to terms by giving up part of a claim

6. funk (103): despondency, gloom, depression

7. imbeciles (103): persons of weak mind

8. tenure (104): conditions or period of holding an office

9. vespiary (104): a nest or colony of social wasps

10. conjugate (107): inflect a verb in its various forms

11. dynamics (114): branch of physics dealing with force or producing an affecting motion; physical or moral forces

12. bigoted (117): blinded by obstinate devotion to a party or creed

13. misdemeanor (117): offense less than a felony

14. felony (117): crime more serious than a misdemeanor; usually punishable in United States by imprisonment for more than a year in a state prison or by death; murder, burglary, and blackmail are felonies

15. hydrochloric (117): compounded of chlorine and hydrogen gas

16. cubism (119): style of painting, drawing, or sculpture developed in the 1900s in which objects are represented by cubes and other geometrical forms rather than by realistic details

17. classical (121): of the highest rank generally, especially of literature or music; refined, chaste, distinguished

18. germination (125): sprouting; starting to grow or develop

19. asphyxiated (126): suffocated because of lack of oxygen in the blood

20. wistful (129): longing, sad, melancholy

Pages 141-198

1. tenacious (142): holding fast; persistent

2. database (142): systemized collection of data that can be easily accessed immediately and manipulated by a data-processing system

3. profoundly (143): strongly, deeply, intensely

4. genetics (146): science dealing with heredity; inherited characteristics

5. dominant (148): most powerful, controlling; designation of dominant genetic characteristic

6. recessive (148): having to do with a recessive (less dominant) genetic characteristic

7. bichon frise (149): a small lively dog with a thick, loosely coiled coat of sold white, or white with patches of gray, orange, or pale yellow

8. muse (152): source of inspiration

9. suffragettes (154): advocate of women's right to vote

10. incriminate (157): involve in an accusation; charge with a crime

11. quantum physics (158): physics according to the quantum theory that whenever radiant energy is transferred, the transfer occurs in pulsations rather than continuously

12. ciao (162): Italian; familiar salutation at meeting or parting; hello or good-bye

13. delinquency (163): offense; failure in a duty; neglect of an obligation

14. graffiti (175): crude drawings or inscriptions on a wall, fence, or other surface

15. indentured servitude (177): an apprentice bound to a master by a sealed document

16. detonate (180): explode with a loud report; set off an explosive

17. perverts (186): persons who practice sexual perversion

18. dormancy (188): state of suspension; not acting

19. shards (195): broken fragments

20. mural (196): wall painting